Icarus Falling Through Light

Riley Villont

BookLeaf Publishing

India | USA | UK

Presentation by *BookLeaf Publishing*

Web: www.bookleafpub.com

E-mail: info@bookleafpub.com

ISBN: 9789363312548

First edition 2024

*For the version of me who didn't think she'd
ever see the sun.*

ACKNOWLEDGEMENT

I would first like to thank Thomas Boyd for being the reason I began writing poetry, this collection would not have happened without your blind belief in my talent. Thank you so much for your faith. Next, I would like to recognize my mother, Christina, for encouraging me to leave my comfort zone and publish. I would also like to acknowledge Kyle Conne, for supporting me and reading through the many rough drafts of these poems. Your friendship has truly changed me and I can not thank you enough.

You and Me at 65 Miles Per Hour

Bright lights reflect
off of exit signs,
mimicking stars
and causing drivers
to go momentarily blind.

Heat rises in waves
causing the asphalt
to appear glistening.

The wind ripples
against my arm
at 65 miles per hour.
The smell
of freshly fallen rain
clings to me
from the velvet air.

In the driver's seat
my best friend sings
off tune to our favorite song;
I sit, tongue-tied,
by the sheer humanness
of it all.

Is this what it means
to feel peace?
To sit in a comfortable
almost silence
with no need
for idle conversation?

To exist in
another person's orbit
without the pressure
to earn your place in it?

There's a warm
thrum settling
in my chest,
rattling my ribs,
and a smile
stamped to my cheeks,
as heat washes
over my face.

We're driving circles
around our town,
this moment,
this night,
this feeling,
will remain never-ending.

Memories of a High School Track

Wind bites at
fingertips and noses,
hair sticks to lips
where it is blown.

The pale blue-gray sky
hangs above
like tap water
pooling around a sink drain.

A song from the 90s
blares in ears.

Red rubber stains
the soles of shoes
as children walk
around and around
and around.

The song in one ear,
a friend's laughter in another;
a blip in a conversation about
death or loss
or God or who knows what.

The song switches.
Around and around
we go.

The Brick Wall

5

Encasing two girls
is a tall brick wall,
built from warped
red clay,
believed to be
indestructible:
unable to fall.

Until it began
to crumble
under the weight
of a growing age
and one by one
the bricks began to rot;

and now,
the bricks
cannot be plastered
together.

The girls
contained by the brick wall
are no more than
strangers.

Death by a Thousand Cuts

The darkest blue
reflects out of your eyes;
the water below crashes against ragged cliffs,
in my chest,
the heart crashes against ribs
just the same.

You encourage me
to dive into unknown depths,
promising that you
will jump with me,

only to leave me to drown
in a moment's notice.
Though you hurt me,
I can't find it in myself
to let you go.

So hold me down
with the weight
of your hollow promises,
I'll let my pain and suffering
be your delight,
just to catch a glimpse
of your smile.

Drag me through fire,
lay me on shattered glass,
or bleed me dry,
and I'll say thank you
simply for your touch.

Murder me with
your sharp stares,
whispered conversations,
and your wit.
Loving you is already
a dagger held to my throat.

You are such
a tragically beautiful monster,
that I can't help
but allow you
to tear me into
a thousand pieces,
so that perhaps,
I can have the
smallest piece of you.

Summer's Tribute

The crackling whistle of fireworks
and the chirping of unlocated frogs
fill my ears,
water ripples around my legs
as my feet kick gently
through diluted chlorine.

The dying sound of laughter
fills the last remnants of open-air
as I am pushed
from my concrete pedestal.

Hair sticks to my skin,
intruding through the corners of my mouth,
as I propel myself towards the surface,
water bubbling from my nose
and rolling down my chin.

Above me, the sky shines
in a burst of blue and yellow
neon light.
This is the
teenage American Dream.

Icarus Falling

Free-falling through air,
scorched by summer's heat.
I am Icarus, falling to my knees.

Yet another mortal
melting their wax wings
for the promise of being freed.

I force myself to soar,
to reach new heights,
confined by the threat
of never seeing light.

I fight the gravity
flinging me towards the sea,
compelled by fright and unease;

if I never reach the light,
the dark will engulf me.
So Icarus flies,
Icarus falls,
because she longs to be seen.

Conversations With a Storm

Salt stings my throat
as I dip beneath violent waters,
thunder crashes like waves,
against the shore,
as lightning flickers
above me in the sky.

A voice comes in,
whirling to wisps
in the wind,
"Be wary of the storm.
What you weather
is what you become."

The waves become stronger,
my breath heaving quicker.
I could, so easily,
fall pliant to the tides.

Yet if I
abandon my flight,
how will I ever
reach new heights?

Hair clings to my face,
sticking to sweat and salt water.

The voice answers,
slow and sultry,
"Is it worth
reaching new heights
if it means,
abandoning your love
for flying?
Glory, my dear,
is not always gold."

My arms begin to grow tired
from fighting the tides,
my body starts to shake
from the trickling cold rain.

Could I desert my journey
if it meant
never exceeding
what is demanded of me?

"Could you surrender
to the waves
if it meant
saving your life?"

Do I desire
glory or life?

"Life is not always
surviving the storm.
Life, more often than not,
is finding laughter
whispered through summer's breeze.
Desire is a craving
often left
unsatisfied."

"You can scratch the itch
until your skin
rips and blood blossoms
into a rose,
till muscle is pulled
from the bone and
that bone is exposed
to the chill of air,
but you will still itch.
You will still yearn
for more."

I nod,
my stomach sinking
as I force myself
to float.

The rain lightens,
the voice dissipates
with the storm.

Autumn's Embers

As the first
leaves of September fall,
I begin to tremble in the cold.

My muse has been lost
to the last cinders
of August,
I have lost my soul.

Do I deserve
any of what has been
awarded to me?

Plans built on that deceit
crumble beneath me,
like ash.

The flame I once
knew and loved
is no more than a weapon
now used against me.

Song of Silence

There's a dead bird
on the side of the road.
It's eyes watching
passersby in a captious stare.

Its wings are crooked,
Its beak left open,
as if it's remarking:
"look at what
humanity has done
to me".

It never asked for life,
never asked for death,
and yet it reveled
as it lived;

and now its voice
has been taken,
a song to be sung
never again.

Its freedom stolen
as swiftly as it was gained.

I find myself
in the bird,
laying dead on my bedroom floor,
wondering if my death will go
unnoticed by those
who attentively
watched me live.

Beaten Wings

Surrounding a golden heat
is a glass pane
thicker than honey.
Lingering inside, a moth,
fluttering its wings.

It flies,
growing frantic the longer
it remains inside;
its wings beating
against the glistening walls,
not knowing the light
means that it has been trapped.

What if,
this is what becomes
of me?

I near the light,
heat surrounds me
in a comforting embrace,
and I am warmed,
and safe.

I beat against the glass,
again and again,
the heat is now searing,
my wings begin to wilt.

I will be another moth
confined in a cage,
victim to its beloved
lights blaze;

and who am I
to attempt an escape
from this tortured fate
that is enclosing on me?

The heat will become sweltering,
the light glaring,
and I will grow weary.

My wings will slow
and I will fall,
but I can not
escape a cage
that has blinded me.

Figures of Nothing

Static shapes buzz
in the fuzzy ceiling
above me;
the fan attached
spinning,
mimicking a hypnotherapy
from the 20th century.

"Who are you?"
Shadows of black
ask from the corners
of my eyes.

"A rotten girl
living a lie."
One of them supplies.

Am I a madman?
I ask the void.

The shadows slink
along the creases
of my eyes.
They say nothing.

Am I a madman?!
I ask again.

The figures laugh,
leaking from my eyes
like water.

Am I a madman?!
Tell me, I plead!

"You are nothing
but a broke girl
with unachievable dreams."
One of their voices
spits the words sharply.

The figures scatter,
their darkness
clouding over the room.

"Why, yes,
you are nothing,
indeed."
Another voice agrees.

A knock interrupts
their menacing cackles,
bringing thick silence
to the room.

Their darkness dissipates
 into static shapes
filling in holes
on the ceiling.

The ceiling fan
continues to spin,
its lights flickering.

On, off,
on, off,
on, off,
on-

Everything stills.

Laying below,
chest rising in strong waves,
my ears ring
in an echo
of the darks' words.

A dead moth and bird
lay with me.

Ophelia's Goodbye

Beyond a meadow,
of poppies and grass overgrown,
is a river,
quaint and quiet.

A girl strolls along the shore,
tears streaking her face,
her wales filling
the empty silence of her songs.

Her hands collect
daisies and violets,
rosemary and pansies,
and a single red poppy;

but as she reaches for the poppy,
at the edge of the bank,
she slips.

The water rushes over her
and instead of fighting the tide,
madness overtakes her mind
and she falls pliant.

She lays,
bouquet in hand,
as the water rushes over her.

She stares at the sun,
a song on her tongue,
as she drowns.

Unknown

I fear the day
the darkness comes;
with no hesitation,
no consideration,
no afterthought.

There will never have been
enough life for me
to feel that I have truly lived.
I will leave a chair empty
at a table for two,
books to be eaten
by dust,
letters with ink
half-dried.
To think that my thoughts
will disintegrate with my skin;
I will never be profound,
I will never be known;
my words fraying like
still, flat hair.

Will my work
become another lost

to the burning of Alexandria,
or a page torn out
forced to go unread?
Another plate scraped off
by a white house
and a chain-link fence?

Words written in warmth and anguish
wiped off the slate
by the 'mighty' and overfed;
deemed unworthy
by those who carve their tongue
with dull words
and flat meaning.

This is the flicker
lurking in the void
that consumes me:
I write of the human burden,
the sweetness and sweat of life,
until my words
lose weight and nourishment.

The darkness will come,
and I will be left,
helpless and alone,
unknown and unfed,
rotting in a life unlived.

Paper People and Steel Streets

The setting sun
washes over the world,
painting the
copper buildings downtown
gold.

One can't help
but become mesmerized,
they forget about
the iron churches
and steel streets
that line our town.

Yet, this town
is growing empty.
The people come to see
the golden buildings,
but the buildings remain empty.

I know my family
will be no different.
The gold buildings
will lose their shine
and my brother'll move

to the city,
my sister to the south.
I will be
the only one left
to this rusting town.

The copper buildings
will erode,
I will be
a paper person
burning in
a metal world.

My Sister, My Brother, and I

My sister is a mess
of chemically red hair
and eyes the color
of the horizon
when a stormy sky
meets the edge
of a field of grass.

She is the mountains
and the fresh fall of snow,
the smell of coffee
and the sound of the late 2000s.

She is driving around town
to get out of our house
and dressing me up
to take me downtown.

My brother is a mess
of curly brown hair
and whiskey.

He is the city,
the smell of gasoline,
the sound of Friday night football games,

and grease stains.

He is horror movies
on a rainy day,
staring at stars,
quiet conversations and existentialism.

I am a mess.
Of red eyes
and ink-stained fingers,
the smell of sun
and vintage book pages.

Yet, my sister and brother
have encompassed so much space
that I don't know
where it leaves me.

Evergreen

Small footsteps
that grow larger in later years,
leaving mud over crisp white snow.
That remains the same.

My dad and brother
covered in sweat and sap,
laying underneath
dark green needles,

a family photographed
in the dim lights
of a barn,
smiles so wide,
people pressed together
so tight,
you can feel the tenderness
radiate off of them.

The past few years
we broke a tradition
and I never imagined
that it would
feel as if I broke too.

None of that love
has been lost,
there have just been
inconveniences,
unfortunate timings,
that come with growing up.

Winter's Heat

Black concrete glimmers
due to melted ice
and headlights set to bright.

In pools of water
on the road's shoulder,
street signs reflect clearly,
a vision coming through at 20/20.

A yellow filter
overtakes the world
when the falling snow
crosses the stream
of dim street lights
in the grayness of night.

The snow catches
on eyelashes
and stray strands of hair,
darkening the color as it melts.

The wind bites
at exposed ears and cheeks,
tinting them the color
of flower buds in the spring.

In the cold,
I feared my beloved fire
would leave me;
but the wind does
not blow out my candle
as long as I hold tight
to its match.

Spring's Awakening

Songs sung in the
break of day
wake me aside
the slightest, dimmest,
light of the sun.

Outside my window,
a robin sits perched
on an empty feeder,
wet with the last
remains of snow.

It sings,
with its head high
and its call loud,
a song I longed
for in the dead
of Winter.

As the season passes,
the song continues,
the sun rises,
its heat grows;
flowers begin to bloom.

Everything is new.

A New Sun

A girl with frayed
brown hair
and eyes the shade
of a storm-filled sky,
stares at the starry night.

From the grass below her,
moisture seeps into
the faded fabric of her jeans;
curling the ends of her hair,
pebbling the backs of her arms
with drops of dew.

All of the versions
of who she was
and who she could become,
lay beside her.

'Who am I?'
She thinks,
'What am I?'

The girls beside her
tell her, one by one,
who they are.

The girl with dusty blue eyes
hates all of them.

Until the youngest,
the wisest,
of them speaks.
"You are whoever
you choose to be."

The girl with dew-soaked hair
sits up and clings
to her knees,
"I can't be me."
She says to herself.

The young girl speaks,
"Then you won't be."

So the girl with moon-struck eyes
speaks to the sky,
"When the sun rises
tomorrow,
I shall not be the girl
I was today,
nor the one from yesterday.
I shall be whoever I choose.
I shall be new.

Wings of Flight

A bird flies
through the black cloak
of night,
scared of what lingers
in the dark.

It must fly
through the night and fear,
its life depends
on the light.

A bird flies
through the rise
of the sun,
wish that it would be gifted
a new start.

Trilling prayers
that the dawn of a new day
marks the start of a new life,
a new adventure,
a new time.

A bird flies
through the afternoon's breeze,

hoping that it's wings
won't grow tired.

The wind,
biting and cruel,
blows against it,
rumpling it's feather,
freezing its beak.

A bird flies
through the sunset,
dreary as it may be,
twittering anxious calls,
excited for the rain to fall.

It knows the rain
in the clouds covering
it's precious sun,
bring sustenance
so that it may live
another day.

A bird rests on a branch
through the night,
knowing the dark
does not mean death.

It finds that the dark offers,
time to rest;

a time to reset.

While the sun
demands action,
the moon assures peace,
the dark soothes
what the light
turns into unease.

A bird is forced to fly
once the sun has risen,
prepared and reluctant for its journey.

Today the air,
is warm,
causing its feathers
to droop,
it to pant,
unfamiliar with the heat.

The bird begs
for the dark to return.

The bird still flies.